~~con~~ temporary ~~archi~~ tecture

Structures of Necessity

Birkhäuser
Basel

With the support of the
Swiss Arts Council
Pro Helvetia

Temporary utilitarian structures have been our obsession since our student days. It started at the end of the 2000s as a collection of snapshots of ephemeral buildings that we saw around us every day. These structures often inspired and intrigued us more than famous architectural icons and monuments. They spellbound us with their lightness and strength, elegance and radicality, monotonicity and beauty. To us, they were initially not a subject of research and analysis, but rather a field for architectural inspiration and discussion about alternative construction techniques.

In 2012, for our first built project as KOSMOS architects, we decided to use "debris netting" as a translucent skin to define the volume of a temporary museum. This material—one of the common materials of temporary infrastructure—is used as a cover for construction site scaffolding. "Construction site materials" were rarely used in construction back then, although they offered great potential for architectural experimentation. Using debris netting reflected the temporality of the project, was affordable within our modest budget, was fast and easy to work with, and could be easily reused on any construction site afterward.

Later, after years of collecting cases in many countries and analyzing them, after multiple workshops and projects where these structures were used as practical references, we came to understand the ingenuity of such structures, their intelligence and innovation, and their resourcefulness. There is plenty to learn from them. To articulate, first of all to ourselves, what we appreciate in them and what contemporary architecture can learn from temporary structures, we decided to organize our observations into a publication.

We continued with an "undeclared manifesto" of these structures, which was presented at the "State of Art in Architecture" exhibition at the Triennale di Milano in February 2020, right before the pandemic, in the form of a huge 1.5-meter album and a lecture. We tried to make the "manifesto" straightforward and visual. While not presenting it as academic research, we aimed to show both our admiration for the subject and the pragmatic ways it can be helpful in the design process.

That manifesto became the basis of the current book. While revising and extending the text, and finalizing the collection of examples (despite its potential infinity), we tried to keep the book's spirit as straightforward and immediate as the structures themselves. Knowing that we are not the only ones interested in this topic, we invited several colleagues and friends to expand the book with a few essays and commentaries, offering different perspectives and points of view. This is how contributions by Jan de Vylder, Charlotte Malterre-Barthes, and Philip Ursprung framed this book.

Artem Kitaev, Leonid Slonimskiy
Co-founders of KOSMOS Architects

decorative
functional

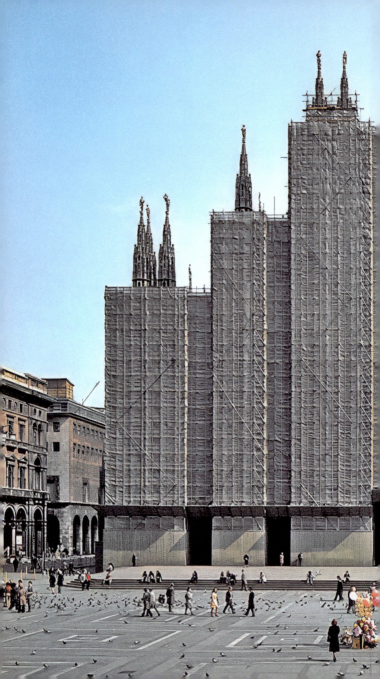

ordinary
unique

Duomo di Milano under renovation, Milan, Italy

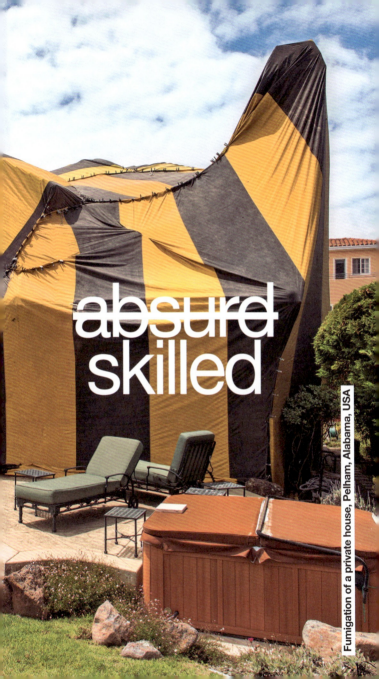

absurd
skilled

Fumigation of a private house, Pelham, Alabama, USA

Printed vinyl banner covering construction and showing a reconstruction, Moscow, Russia

hopeless
powerful

Monument to Princess Olga, the Apostle Andrew, St. Cyril and St. Methodius, protected by sandbags, Kyiv, Ukraine, March 2022

maximum effect minimum means

Bauprofile (outlines of a future building volume), Zurich, Switzerland

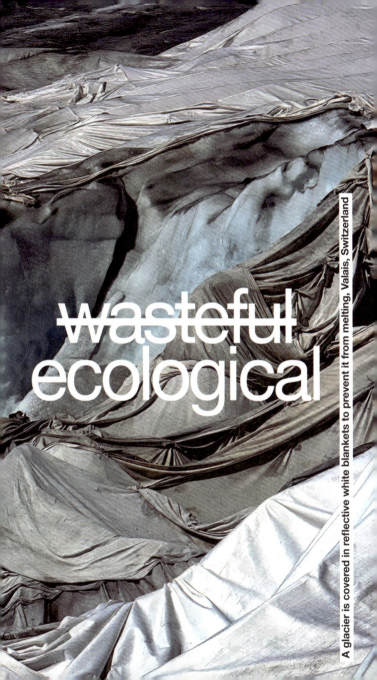

~~wasteful~~
ecological

A glacier is covered in reflective white blankets to prevent it from melting, Valais, Switzerland

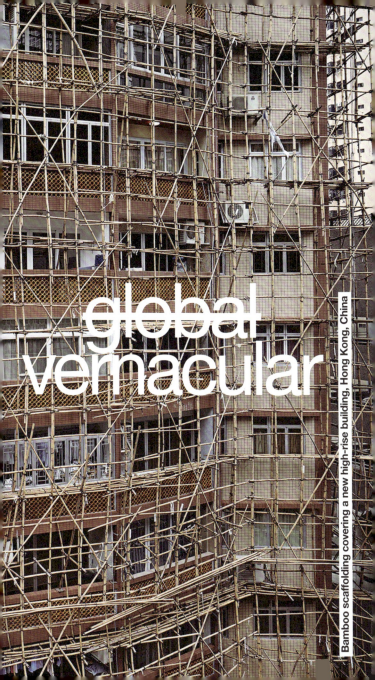

global
vernacular

Bamboo scaffolding covering a new high-rise building, Hong Kong, China

Learning from the existing landscape is a way of being revolutionary for an architect.[1]

1   Robert Venturi, Denise Scott Brown, and Steven Izenour, *Learning from Las Vegas* (Cambridge, MA: The MIT Press, 1972), 3.

Architecture as a reflection of our society facilitates the development and transformation of our community.

Following the transition from an industrial to an informational society, traditional methods of construction lack the rapidity and flexibility necessary to respond to the changing needs of our society. These new challenges—social, economic, political, environmental, technological, and climatic—are pressing the architecture and construction disciplines to change. However, this change hardly happens, and even if it does, it cannot adapt to the pace of the transformation of the contemporary world.

Utilitarian temporary structures, which are built of necessity and designed to be easily assembled and disassembled, respond to changes in needs in the most direct way. They deserve to be looked at and analyzed as a snapshot of reality, an immediate reflection of actual problems and societal demands.

Temporary architecture is an important element of the infrastructure. This mute urban layer ensures the functioning of multiple processes in the city, from construction and deconstruction to maintenance, guidance, and protection. It substitutes for the functionality of architecture when there are no resources or time for permanent construction. These permanently present, temporary elements create a visual identity along with architecture and landscape. Yet due to their categorization as temporary, they almost remain invisible to the public. For the same reason, they lack consideration and reflection by architects, theorists, and urban designers.

What could architecture learn from temporary structures? In a series of essays combined in the publication ~~con~~temporary ~~archi~~tecture we will explore this question.

Ideal City vs. Real City: Parallel Realities

The series of early Renaissance Italian paintings depict the utopic "La Città Ideale"—the Ideal City—as imagined in the humanistic philosophy of his time. Streets and squares in the images consist of purely architectural objects—harmoniously designed and well-proportioned houses, facades, fountains, and churches. The city looks unusually sterile and does not carry any traces of urban life or human activity. The ideal city, being conceived in accordance with the dictates of the rational and moral objective, is entirely architectural. It does not leave space for the appearance of any extra, random, temporary, or nondesigned urban layers.

In contrast to that utopian vision, an image of any contemporary, busy, and active city shows that a substantial part of its urban landscape is constituted of various infrastructural and temporary structures that support and cover architecture, define borders, provide security, maintenance, directions, advertisement, protection from the environment, fire safety, and facilitate transportation.

These structures play an important role in the urban quotidian life, facilitating it and being present physically, but at the same time, often stay unnoticed and almost invisible. As mentioned in Robert Venturi's and Denise Scott Brown's *Learning from Las Vegas*, "Signs inflect toward the highway even more than buildings."[1]

The same happens with auxiliary and temporary structures, which can sometimes visually, spatially, and even technically impact cities more than permanent buildings. Nevertheless, due to their ephemeral and utilitarian character, these structures are almost excluded from both the field of architectural discourse and the public's perception. Being purely utilitarian, these objects are free from aesthetic judgment and cultural influence. That makes these structures freer than traditional, designed architecture and eventually more innovative, both technologically and aesthetically.

Architects have always been inspired and influenced by technology: Le Corbusier referred to machines and ships in his architecture;[2] Walter Gropius, to factories and industrial architecture.[3] Industrial buildings and structures have always been symbols of brave and innovative spatial compositions. The naked functionality of these structures based on purely technical requirements triggered many architectural movements and design ideas. Nevertheless, nowadays industrial buildings are packed in more compact and generic volumes and even one of the most technological manufacturing plants of today—the Tesla Giga factory in Nevada—does not offer any new, inspiring formal language.

On the contrary, temporary infrastructure, being excluded from the sphere of architectural interest, has kept its roughness and straightforwardness. Its aesthetic is fair to its structural meaning. Temporariness and short construction time allow it to use the latest achievements of technologies in structural as well as material aspects. These structures give insight today into what architecture will look like tomorrow and show us what contemporary architecture can learn from temporary structures. This is why we titled the book ~~con~~temporary ~~archi~~tecture.

1   Robert Venturi, Denise Scott Brown, and Steven Izenour, *Learning from Las Vegas* (Cambridge, MA: The MIT Press, 1972), 51.

2   "The house is a machine for living in." Le Corbusier, *Towards a New Architecture*, trans. Frederick Etchells (London: John Roker, 1931), 4.

3   Walter Gropius, "The Development of Modern Industrial Architecture, 1913," in *Form and Function: A Source Book for the History of Architecture and Design 1890–1939*, ed. Tim Benton, Charlotte Benton, and Dennis Sharp (London: Crosby Lockwood Staples, 1975), 54–55.

The painting *La Città Ideale* by an unkown artist from Central Italy

A street in Hong Kong, China

What is ~~Con~~temporary ~~Archi~~tecture?

A̶R̶C̶H̶ITECTURE

By definition, architecture, with its root *archi—* (Greek: chief, main) has an author and, therefore, authority. In the case of anonymous infrastructural buildings and temporary structures, a better definition would be merely *tecture* (from the Greek *tekton*: builder). The word *anonymous* is not used in its exact sense because almost every structure has an author—even if the author is unknown. The anonymity reflects the attitude rather than the factual absence of an author. Anonymous buildings are free from the political views, religion, ethnicity, and psychology of the author, and therefore distill their meaning to the structure.

C̶O̶N̶TEMPORARY

The temporary character of tecture adds another coordinate—the time component—to the subject. Entering into a short-term relationship with the context, this type of construction manifests itself as an event, an intervention. Temporary structures are not trying to appropriate, consume, or complete their context. That is yet another reason why tecture is almost absent in the professional architectural and historical discourse. At the same time, speed of assembly allows temporary structures to use the most recent construction technologies and address the latest challenges of assembly on-site. Often, this makes temporary structures more innovative and daring than modern, long-term construction developments.

TECTURE IS ESSENTIAL

Tecture is born out of need and necessity; it serves solely utilitarian purposes. Tecture emerges in situations when a permanent building would take too long to be built. It appears when there is a need to repair, to construct, to advertise, or to protect. It strictly adheres to the "form follows function" formula and achieves its goal with the minimum of means. Delivering required functionality, tecture is never judged from an aesthetic point of view. It does not appear for representation, fun, or someone's political ambitions. It exists while the problem exists and gets disassembled as soon as the problem is solved. If there is no urgent need for tecture, there is no tecture. The practicality of tecture in that case defines its environmental responsibility.

TECTURE IS MINIMAL

The engineer Mikhail Koshkin used to say: "The best detail … is the one which doesn't exist." This describes well the logic of its functionality: the detail that does not exist will never break, does not require any maintenance, and will not raise construction costs. Tecture is a spatial imprint of function and economy. Because it does not serve any representational function, the goals of tecture are achieved by the most resource- and cost-efficient and minimal way. The aspect of beauty is excluded from the tecture's morphology and therefore it creates a special type of aesthetics, its own beauty.

Cost and resource efficiency make tecture ecological. It is inherently sustainable and often follows the logic of the circular economy. The materials and whole structures are often reused, such as prefabricated and industrial scaffolding, nets, and other thin membranes. These are used in the most minimal quantities and made purposefully adjustable, reusable, deflatable. No one decides to ship tecture from thousands of kilometers away—it is used locally, therefore it has a low carbon footprint. It occupies minimal space while hardly leaving a trace in the environment after being disassembled.

TECTURE IS CONTEMPORARY

Tecture is an agent to solve a problem immediately. It deals with an actual problem using actual tools. On average, it takes about seven years in Europe to design and build a building. That means the moment the building is complete, the design and technologies are already outdated: it is a several-year-old design that solves a problem of the people who used to live there based on outdated technologies.

Tecture is a snapshot of reality, which represents problems, achievements, and facilities of the actual moment.

We live in a rapidly changing world: economically, climatically, politically, culturally. Architecture takes too long to build, and in some cases, by the time the project is designed, all the permissions are received, and the structure is finally built, reality has changed so much that a newly completed building has to undergo a renovation. In that sense, tecture, being a direct tool to solve particular issues, is much more flexible and much more appropriate to meet the challenges of nowadays and the future.

TECTURE IS FREE

Architecture is imprisoned by law. Architecture is controlled by city regulations, safety requirements, preservation committees, and procedures of public authorizations. Most architectural regulations are not applied to temporary structures and therefore, they are much freer and independent, both spatially and aesthetically. What would be totally unacceptable as a permanent structure is completely fine when labeled "temporary."

The fact that no one takes notice of it is the reason for its development potential. Due to the speed of its construction, affordability, and reusability, tecture is a perfect polygon for future architecture. The temporary character of such structures allows one to test radical architectural solutions in the city: buildings of enormous scale, windowless surfaces, iconic geometries, interference with the flow of people, striking colors. Through tecture, we can see how little we need to achieve a certain goal or how much will be accepted by the context. Tecture shows the potential future (or, one can argue, death) of architecture without manifesting an ambitious goal in the conventional sense.

TECTURE IS HONEST

Architecture is regulated by beauty: apart from other qualities, it is supposed to be beautiful—to represent either the individual or common vision of beauty. However, the notion of beauty takes a backseat to technological progress. Everything truly new looks ugly in a conventional perception. We as society need time to understand unfamiliar concepts and reset our aesthetical perception. With time, architecture appropriates achievements of technologies, digesting them and releasing them as new standards of beauty. Tecture is not bound by requirements of beauty, and directly uses the most efficient way to solve a problem: that way it is often the most innovative and honest.

Being beautiful is often the equivalent to being conservative, and in order to conform to the conventions of beauty, architecture fakes itself. Many new materials simulate traditional finishes instead of declaring their original appearance. For instance, even though a typical building wall today consists of several layers, architects are still trying to hide them and pretend the wall is made out of a solid material like hundreds of years ago. This happens in wall cladding, false ceilings, fake facade elements, and imitative finishes. Most of the elements of classical architecture were initially parts of the building structure or technology of its manufacturing. With time, the reasoning behind those purely utilitarian methods of assembly was lost. The methods were aestheticized and became an obligatory set of architectural rules and applied decorations. Since then, these details play only a symbolic, decorative role, but they lay the foundation for Vitruvius's formulae of stability, utility, and beauty, or Louis Sullivan's principle "form follows function," and other classical formulae of architecture.[1] Interestingly enough, the same happens in modern and minimalist buildings, when architects fake continuous concrete slabs by rendering false ceilings with cement, hiding the way the building is really made. This dishonesty and pretentiousness occurs due to the discrepancy between the architectural style and the technologies used to create the building.

In contrast to architecture, tecture is honest. Each element of the structure is placed out of need; color and material are assigned because of the element's function. It uses the achievement of technical progress and does not hesitate to reveal the role of each element. Elements never pretend to play another role. The logic of tecture is rational, clear, and honest.

---

1   The architect Louis Sullivan coined the maxim, which refers to Viollet-le-Duc's theories: "a rationally designed structure may not necessarily be beautiful but no building can be beautiful that does not have a rationally designed structure."

Conditions
of Necessity

One of the most essential aims of architecture is to accommodate required spatial functionality using available material resources and time. Temporary solutions are the most practical way to solve the problem now, before a permanent solution is developed and constructed. However, temporary structures should not be perceived exclusively as quick substitutes for permanent architecture: often, temporality is a necessary quality of a structure that will be assembled and disassembled due to the temporary nature of the need. Seasonal infrastructure, solutions for temporary events, immediate responses to natural disasters, and temporary scaffolding for construction are regularly and repeatedly used temporary solutions. These temporary structures gain permanent significance. In this context, it is difficult to draw a line between permanent and temporary architecture: often, temporary structures, or those assembled with the understanding that they will be disassembled in the future, remain on site longer than "permanent" architecture, which is erected with the intention to stay for decades, with the material potential to last for ages. From an environmental point of view, lightweight structures that respond to current needs and can be efficiently reused elsewhere feature a significantly more vital type of architecture. Principles of temporary architecture could inform "permanent" design.

Comprehension of architecture as a process requires understanding any structure not as a final design, but as one of many configurations of built material on the site. The inevitability of changing demands and contexts requires a shift in the design paradigm from designing for a specific program to designing for future adaptations. Temporary structures present a great example of reliable practical solutions, able to change and transform according to new demands or disappear if the delivered functionality is no longer needed, keeping their resources available for further use and interpretation.

Environmental challenges place resources, their availability, and their impact at the center of professional discourse, offering an opportunity to revisit the practice of temporary construction and reusable structures as a possible response to current challenges and potential inspiration for architecture.

Temporary structures and solutions are used in almost all spheres of the built environment and accommodate a great diversity of needs. The application of temporary solutions is so ubiquitous and diverse that any categorization seems incomplete. In this publication, we propose to organize temporary structures into seven groups, or "conditions." This grouping is obviously not exhaustive but allows us to define the most impactful, in our opinion, spheres of application of temporary structures: construction, fake, climate, safety, event, protection, and vernacular.

Conditions of Necessity:

Construction
Fake
Climate
Safety
Event
Protection
Vernacular

Construction

"There is nothing more permanent than temporary." This proverb very precisely describes the role of temporary structures in urban development and architecture. A fast, practical solution sometimes stays much longer than initially planned. Historical and developing cities are in a constant mode of self-repair, maintenance, or growth. In his book *How Buildings Learn*, Stewart Brand states: "all buildings grow."[1] Therefore, tools of urban transformation—construction sites and scaffolding—contribute a great deal to the image of any city.[2]

As tourists, we travel around the world to see the same iconic views that have been reproduced thousands of times in photographs, postcards, social media posts, and other media. Yet in reality, monuments constantly need repair and are often covered in construction nets and scaffolding: a common reason for sad tourist selfies in front of a wrapped Big Ben or covered San Marco cathedral. Ironically, it is exactly those temporary structures that create a specific notion and make the visit unique.

The scale and importance of preservation escalates each year, along with the number of preserved and listed buildings (as Rem Koolhaas mentions in *Cronocaos*).[3] Can we imagine that in the future, when most cities are fully built and preserved, the only free domain left for architects will be temporary structures?

Besides impacting a city's image, construction sites also reflect the economic conditions of the moment: lots of quickly growing sites show an economy on the rise—for example, in Hong Kong, where Peter Steinhauer shot his famous *Cocoons* photo series. Old and worn-out scaffolding throughout the city reflects long and complex (re)construction projects or, on a larger scale, stagnation in the economy.

The development of scaffolding has always been tightly connected to the development of engineering and practical areas of construction such as military and nautical technologies and civil engineering.

Scaffolding has helped architects overcome architectural restrictions and perform unique superhuman tasks. The most famous examples are the construction of St. Peter's Basilica and erection of the Vatican obelisk in Rome, and the construction of St. Isaac's Cathedral and erection of the Alexander Column in St. Petersburg.

The columns of St. Peter's Basilica in Rome and the Vatican obelisk were erected with technologies developed by master builder Nicola Zabaglia (among others). These construction techniques were derived from shipbuilding, where similar hoists and levers were used to raise masts and sails.

During the construction of the Alexander Column at Dvortsovaya Square in St. Petersburg by Auguste de Montferrand, military construction techniques were used, developed by Agustín de Betancourt, a famous army general and civil engineer. More than 2,000 soldiers and 400 workers were employed to lift up the 600-ton monument.[4]

A real structural challenge and minimal budget for temporary scaffolding, together with the absence of any representational or aesthetical limitations, allow engineers and architects to push the envelope of technical innovation and reveal real achievements of the construction industry of the moment.

Interestingly, the expression of historical scaffolding on antique engravings looks unusually modern for its time. Aesthetically, these relate more to contemporary architecture of the twentieth and twenty-first centuries than to the classicist or baroque structures that they brought to life. Sometimes, utilitarian structures foreshadow the development of architecture better than futuristic design utopias.

1   Stewart Brand, *How Buildings Learn: What Happens After They're Built* (New York: Penguin Books, 1994), 10.
2   Brand, *How Buildings Learn*, 10.
3   Rem Koolhaas, "Preservation Is Overtaking Us," *Future Anterior* 1, no. 2 (Fall 2004): 1–3.
4   A. Ricard de Montferrand, *Plans et détails du monument consacré à la mémoire de l'Empereur Alexandre* (Paris: Chez Thierry Frères, 1836).

Tecture used (and continues) to use the most cutting-edge construction techniques; in this case—from military engineering.

Installation of columns of St. Isaac's Cathedral, 1830, lithograph from a drawing by A. de Montferrand, 1845

Imp. y...

VUE DE L'ÉDIFICE ENTO...

Aesthetically, the scaffolding structures have to do with modern architecture much more than with the classicist or baroque structures that came to life thanks to scaffolding.

Pl. 34

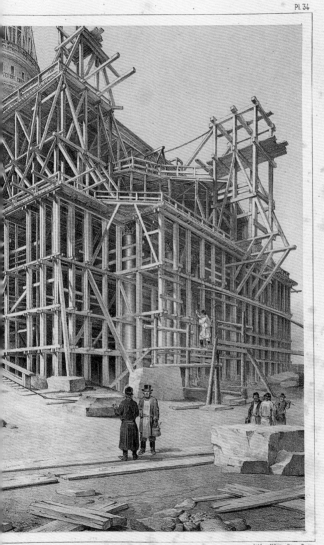

Lith par Villemin Fig par Bayot.

...S SES CHARPENTES.

St. Isaac's Cathedral, surrounded by all its scaffolding, drawing from the album of A. de Montferrand, 1845

Tecture has helped architects perform unique superhuman tasks such as the erection of enormous monuments.

Erection of the Vatican obelisk in Rome, Italy. Drawing by Carlo Fontana. Engraved by Alessandro Specchi

Construction of the Merefa-Kherson bridge in Dnipro, Ukraine, 21 December 1932

Scaffolding for the Lusail Visitor
Center, Doha, Qatar, 2017

Taipei Performing Arts Center by OMA under construction, Taipei, Taiwan

Ideally spherical shape of the Taipei performing center by OMA covered with a simple and practical pitched roof of tecture.

The Big Buddha statute under maintenance at the
Po Lin Monastery in Ngong Ping, Hong Kong, China

What is totally unacceptable as a permanent structure is completely fine when labeled "temporary."

Duomo di Milano under restoration, Milan, Italy

Hotel Astoria under renovation, Leipzig, Germany

Saint-François, restoration, Geneva, Switzerland

Heating of the construction site during winter, Zurich, Switzerland

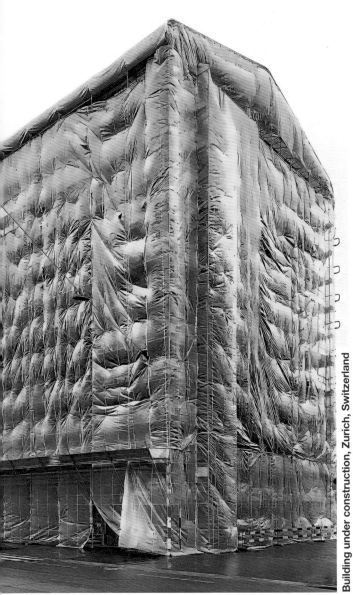

Building under construction, Zurich, Switzerland

New building under construction, Hong Kong, China

New building under construction, Hong Kong, China

Restoration of the The Motherland Calls monument, Volgograd, Russia

Monuments require constant and meticulous maintenance and sometimes are covered in tecture for years: a common reason for tourists' disappointment.

Restoration of the St. Mark's Basilica, Venice, Italy

However, exactly these temporary structures make the iconic buildings have unique and changing appearances.

Big Ben and the Houses of Parliament under restoration, London, England

Colosseum under restoration, Rome, Italy

Minimal additions: transparent film and wooden posts transform the purely symbolic structure of a classicist fountain into a functional workers' pavilion.

Renovation of a monument, Moscow, Russia

Using full-length wooden logs
as temporary props is a unique
Swiss tecture typology.

Construction of the Hochhaus H1 Zwhatt-Areal in Regensdorf by Boltshauser Architekten, Switzerland

Church of the Apostles Peter and Paul under restoration, Peterhof, Saint-Petersburg, Russia

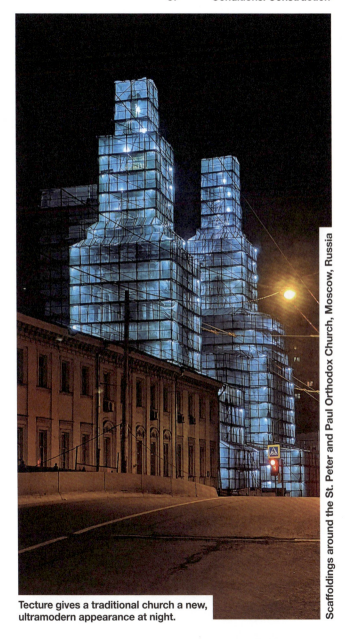

Scaffoldings around the St. Peter and Paul Orthodox Church, Moscow, Russia

Tecture gives a traditional church a new, ultramodern appearance at night.

Badaevskiy Brewery redevelopment, Moscow, Russia

Openings that allow the wind to pass through the textile on a windy seafront create their own architectural language. This practical response to local climatic challenges features a truly vernacular approach to architecture.

Construction site in Porto, Portugal

Fake

Printed vinyl banner covering construction and showing a reconstruction, Moscow, Russia

The development and popularization of large-scale printing technologies has led to the appearance of printed architecture, a relatively new typology of tecture in which whole buildings are covered by vinyl membranes with prints of the real facade hidden behind it. Despite the neoteric technology of this invention, the concept of replacing real architecture with an image that indicates only the necessary elements of a building or landscape was introduced a long time ago.

One of the most famous examples of painted architecture (the historical equivalent of printed architecture) is the concept of the Potemkin villages. According to legend,[1] in 1787, famous Russian politician Grigory Potemkin—in order to impress Russian Empress Catherine II on her visit to the newly conquered territories of the south of the Russian Empire—erected fake villages along the way the empress traveled. The fake facades of houses drawn on flat surfaces and installed in the landscape simulated recently constructed flourishing villages. Even though this story is assumed to be a myth, the idea of faking architecture or even urban developments, an analog to augmented reality, has been repeated many times.

In contemporary history, we can find a wide range of examples of Potemkin villages, with different levels of abstraction and absurdity, in different parts of the world. Often, fake architecture appears on the occasion of political events or celebrations on a grand scale, when local authorities look for the most efficient way to visually improve the place they are responsible for.

The 39th G8 Summit was held in Northern Ireland in June 2013. Preparing their towns for international guests, local councils decided to decorate dilapidated houses and abandoned buildings with colorful prints on a one-to-one scale.[2] In creative ways, different sizes of falsification were combined. The windows of abandoned shops were covered with blooming images of prosperous butcher shops, bakeries, and local businesses. Photos of well-renovated houses, heritage, and landscape masked entire streets in some towns.

Another example can be found in Ufa, a provincial city in Russia, which hosted the summits of the SCO (Shanghai Cooperation Organisation) and BRICS (Brazil, Russia, India, China, and South Africa) in 2015. The local administration was not able to repair and restore old buildings, clean up dumps, and plant trees, and therefore decided to massively reproduce fake historical facades, seemingly impressive office buildings (with blue skies reflected in the windows) and even grass fields and forested landscapes.[3] It was exceptionally absurd due to the naive, low-resolution, or highly photoshopped stock images that were chosen for the prints.

Sometimes, fake temporary facades are located in place of the reconstructed historical buildings, which make the reconstruction of historical monuments "unnoticeable." Radical and inappropriate reconstructions and the demolition of historically important monuments often take place behind those shields with classical windows, balustrades, and ornaments without any possibility of public control. Funnily enough, false facades use the same technology as commercial banners. Printed architecture is a coating of construction sites with a commercial promise of successful accomplishment of the restoration process or a new development.

The printed banners stretched over surfaces of the building are probably the most radical expression of fake architecture. Nowadays, when the responsibility of architects is often limited to the facade design of a maximized square-meter-efficient urban volume provided by the developer, it actually makes sense to use the most efficient and practical tool for it—printing technologies.

The concept of false facades and simulation in architecture is broadly and globally used: from Venetian cathedrals with marble front facades and brickwork on the side facades of the building to typical western saloons, where a decorated thin surface of the main "flat-roof" facade is installed in front of a pitched-roof barn-like volume of the building. This type of architecture was defined by Robert Venturi and Denise Scott Brown in *Learning from Las Vegas* as "decorated sheds"—a remarkable example of the balance between technology and architecture, economic efficiency, and representation.[4]

Historically, fake architecture was present particularly in interiors and ranged from the literal representation of sky and heaven gardens in the domes and ceilings of Christian churches to drawn fake doors, decoration, or even materials in peasant houses. One of the extreme examples of graphical simulation in architecture could be found in the Monastery of San Niccolò in Prato, Italy. Here, columns of marble were painted with a "marble pattern" in another color. One of the abbots of the monastery did not like the color of the marble columns, but admitted the representational quality of marble, so he ordered that fake marbling be painted over the real marble to make the color trendier.

Although traditionally Potemkin villages have a negative connotation, it is interesting to look at building wraps as an instrument of architectural falsification.

The printed facade—is it the death or the future of architecture? How much do we actually need "architecture" if a 1-mm-thick surface with a digital print can substitute for a whole building in a historical center for years? If the print can inform us about the functional content of the building, about the shapes of the windows and pretty realistically represent the materials of the facade, whereas purely functional structures behind it will provide floor areas, circulation, and protection from the elements, would it be possible to live in a printed city? Can facades be completely detached from the buildings' content or should they actually represent the organization of life behind it?

Facades—just like clothes—represent the philosophy or status of its owner: company, city, or private person. Clothes (being the main part of the fashion industry) should cope with the latest trends and styles. The speed of rotation of architectural and design trends nowadays is comparable to the fashion industry, but with an important difference: the speed of manufacturing the "outfit" for a building is significantly longer. This system produces "last-season houses"—those that are just completed already have an outdated design. Apart from this, buildings require aesthetical renovation much earlier as construction materials are damaged or are in physical need of repair. This causes high ecological detriments to the architectural industry.

In contemporary cities, where buildings are often renovated or rebuilt every twenty years or sooner, should we actually waste real materials? Or could "fake" prints provide enough beauty and political or cultural representation to the buildings?

Architects could probably learn from fake facades that allow buildings to significantly change their appearance with a minimum of means while preserving the main structure. The idea of building components' different time spans by Stewart Brand is crucial for circularity in building construction.[5]

1   Aleksandr Panchenko, *O russkoi istorii i kul´ture* (St. Petersburg: Azbuka, 2000), 416.
2   Cathal McNaughton, Reuters. "A Dilapidated Irish Whiskey Town Is Painting Its Vacant Shops to Look Full," *Business Insider*, August 30, 2013, https://www.businessinsider.com/bushmills-ireland-paints-empty-storefronts-for-tourism-2013-8.
3   Ilya Varlamov, "How Ufa Is Preparing for the SCO and BRICS Summits," July 3, 2015, https://varlamov.ru/1393217.html.
4   Robert Venturi, Denise Scott Brown, and Steven Izenour, *Learning from Las Vegas* (Cambridge, MA: The MIT Press, 1972), 90.
5   Stewart Brand's six layers of building that age at different rates. See Steward Brand, *How Buildings Learn: What Happens after They're Built* (New York: Penguin Books, 1994), 13.

The Supreme Court is a building too representative to stay without a face during the sandblasting and restoration works.

United States Supreme Court building, Washington, D.C., US

Printed facade, Moscow, Russia

False facades during the 7th BRICS summit,
Ufa, Russia, July 2015

Tecture is the most minimal way to
create a visual trompe-l'œil: fake
historical facades, fake blue skies,
fake window reflections, fake forests.

Another level of falsification: printed greenery, Ufa, Russia, July 2015

Even grass fields and forested landscapes were printed. The decisions were taken rapidly: naive, low-resolution, or highly photoshopped stock images were chosen for prints.

Fake storefronts installed for the G8 Summit, Bushmills, Northern Ireland, United Kingdom

Fake tecture helps to hide shady demolitions and nontransparent reconstruction projects. Carefully drawn, this banner covers a void left after the demolition of a building.

Banner covering a construction site in Moscow, Russia

This shopping mall with a fake
facade of the Hermitage Palace
preceded the real one by five years.

Fake facade, Moscow, Russia

Printed facades make us question how
much we actually need architecture
if a 1-mm-thin printed surface
can substitute a whole building in
a historical center for years?

Printed facade, Moscow, Russia

Printed facade, Moscow, Russia

A palimpsest of fake, real, and
temporary architectures

Printed facade, Moscow, Russia

Climate

The Rhone Glacier, covered with blankets to prevent melting, Valais, Switzerland

The climate on our planet is rapidly changing, and we live in a constant state of emergency, with which architecture cannot cope due to its slowness.[1] Tecture, by virtue of its quick construction methods, has become the best tool of dealing with landscape and climatic issues. Initially, the purpose of architecture was to protect humans from nature. Ironically enough, now we are developing structures to protect and preserve nature from the human impact and from itself.

Tecture probably returns us to the initial meaning of architecture: facilitating the coexistence of humans and nature (even under extreme conditions).

We use the term *landscape tecture* to define all types of infrastructure that are used to solve or improve landscape and climatic issues. This term includes infrastructure of different types: for agricultural needs; against the effects of natural disasters and global warming; or for the creation of artificial landscapes.

In a way, landscape infrastructure creates an artificial nature: alternative, human-made landscape. Even though we sometimes perceive it as a contradiction to nature, adjusting the landscape is an essential quality to all organisms on Earth. Human-made landscape reveals the natural beauty of the planet Earth the same way as anthills, birds' nests, or spider webs. Human-made structures are often alien to their surroundings, but it is indeed very difficult to draw a line to separate originally natural landscapes and nature created by the inhabitants of Earth. With the constantly growing population on the planet, when human impact is inevitable, should we stop perceiving Earth as a wild forest and rather think of it as a well-treated garden? In reality, the romantic beauty of a landscape and pristine nature is a constructed dream. "Nature" nowadays is a highly complex, artificially supported, human-made machine. The infrastructure that supports nature is actually another, less visible landscape in itself, one that is rarely acknowledged or highlighted. We believe that it is important to reflect on this hidden layer as a new type of nature. The mechanism of nature engineering consists of irrigation systems, snow cannons, avalanche protection, weather stations, solar panels, water pipes, electrical networks, and many other variations of landscape tecture.

GLOBAL WARMING

Our planet is getting warmer, and glaciers around the world are shrinking continuously. In the Alpine region the big glaciers are retreating by 30 to 40 meters each year.[2] According to a study led by the University of Fribourg in 2017, 90 percent of some of the biggest Swiss glaciers might disappear by the year 2100.[3] In the Rhone region, for example, that shrinking represents an economic emergency as well as an environmental one. The ice mass that covered a major part of Switzerland 11,500 years ago, and especially the ice grotto that has been carved into the ice for visitors to walk through, are significant tourist attractions. The glacier has retreated by 1,400 meters and has shrunk by 350 meters in ice thickness since 1856.[4] That's why the most vulnerable parts of the glacier, especially the grotto inside it, are covered in blankets made of heavy-duty fleece material from spring until autumn (covering approximately 20,000 square meters). The blankets, their white color chosen to reflect light before it strikes the ice, may slow the glacier's decline. Yet the glacier still loses 10 to 12 centimeters on a hot day. There is a certain level of absurdity and contradiction in the attempt to save the glacier from melting (which will happen anyway) and the fact that the blankets were placed there to save a tourist attraction—a cave in the glacier—rather than the glacier itself.

FLOODS
Acqua alta is a recurring phenomenon in Venice, especially in November and the winter months. In recent years, exceptionally high tides have become more common. On these occasions, the city provides elevated wooden walkways in areas of the city that are prone to flooding. The bridges are constructed from wooden modules. All stores have glass barricades on their doorsteps. During the floods, it is also common to use sandbag barricades. These bags are placed on top of each other, then untied on the side facing the tide.

RECLAIMED LAND
The island Koh Panyee in Thailand is a small fishing village that consists primarily of fishing boats and small houses on stilts around steep, uninhabited rock. Almost the entire inhabited part of the island is artificial land. The scarcity of land excludes any

noncommercial public space or sport facilities on the island. Inspired by FIFA World Cup 1986, a group of Koh Panyee boys decided to found their own football team for which they built a floating football pitch. The first pitch was built out of old fishing cages and the remains of wood construction. With time, Panyee FC became one of the most successful youth football clubs in the south of Thailand, and the old pitch was replaced by a new one, built out of floating tecture—pontoon blocks. This temporary spatial transformation has led to a big social shift: Koh Panyee is no longer just a small fishing village, but a recognized community with high achievements in sports.

SUN PROTECTION

In agriculture, it is common to use semitransparent fabric—which creates a parallel landscape with improved conditions for vegetation, thus requiring less land and time. It is a "better" nature to cope with human needs.

Protection from direct sun is also relevant in cities and urban areas. In order to protect parking lots from the burning sun in South Asia and South America, suspended "ceilings" of debris netting of different colors are installed. They beautifully filter the light and create unique colored atmospheres in parking lots throughout a city.

In the case of climate change, the enormous scale of undergoing changes (floods, fields, glaciers) is compensated by the elemental quality of tecture. It creates an alternative environment of upgraded or hacked nature.

1   Valérie Masson-Delmotte, Panmao Zhai, et al., eds., *Climate Change 2021: The Physical Science Basis. Contribution of Working Group I to the Sixth Assessment Report of the Intergovernmental Panel on Climate Change* (Cambridge: Cambridge University Press, 2021).

2   "Glacier Case," *International Rights of Nature Tribunal*, https://www.rightsofnaturetribunal.org/cases/glacier-case/#1590541 122764-4235cbab-d351, accessed April 1, 2024.

3   Harry Zekollari, Matthias Huss, and Daniel Farinotti, "Modelling the Future Evolution of Glaciers in the European Alps under the EURO-CORDEX RCM Ensemble," *The Cryosphere* 13, no. 4 (2019): 1125–46, https://doi.org/10.5194/tc-13-1125-2019.

4   Nina Larson, "Blankets Cover Swiss Glacier in Vain Effort to Halt Icemelt," *Phys.org*, September 15, 2015, https://phys.org/news/2015-09-blankets-swiss-glacier-vain-effort.html.

A glacier is covered in reflective white blankets to prevent it from melting, Sölden, Austria

The Rhone Glacier, including the grotto inside it, is covered with blankets made of heavy-duty material from spring until autumn.

A glacier is covered in reflective white blankets to prevent it from melting, Valais, Switzerland

Tecture as a climate agent: urban ceilings in tropical Bangkok protect parked cars from overheating. As a consequence of a pragmatic solution, beauty comes into play: filtered light creates unique colored atmospheres.

Parking lot under a ceiling of debris netting in Bangkok, Thailand

Elevated bridges during Venice's acqua alta create alternative pedestrian routes in the city, offering the bare minimum to get from point A to point B.

Pedestrian footbridges in Venice, Italy

Human-made alternative landscape conditions are "improved" nature for agriculture.

Field covered in landscape textile, Tirol, Austria

Industrial textile protecting the road from falling stones and landslides, Eisenburg, Switzerland

Agricultural tecture in Ama, Oki District, Shimane, Japan

Tecture shows that most efficient solutions are the most elementary.

Sandbag barricades against floods in Moscow, Russia

Tecture naturally refers to human
scale: each element's weight
allows it to be carried by a human.

Preparation for the flood, filling sandbags, Jefferson City, Missouri, USA, July 1993

Sandbag barricade during flooding of the Red River, Fargo, North Dakota, USA, April 2011

Sandbag barricade during flooding, Hendrum, Minnesota, USA, March 2009

Pontoons, originally tecture for ports, create new land: temporary artificial nature.

Floating football field, Koh Panyee, Thailand

Safety

Sidewalk shed, New York, USA

"Safety first." This cliché says a lot about the role that safety infrastructure plays in building design. Regardless of an architect's initial design intent, safety requirements usually come out on top as a separate demand. These are the elements that protect people from being hurt by structures and protect structures from being damaged by people.

They are materialized as independent structures, elements on facades and roofs or inside buildings. They could be as small as anti-bird spikes, as bright as orange protective mats, as massive as concrete blocks. All these elements are rarely designed by architects, but they inevitably appear in the city space.

Safety tecture elements are purely functional, yet this functionality creates a certain visual poetry as well—a functional ornament to an existing building. These elements have a particular visual style: shapes are iconic, memorable, and easy to recognize—simple geometric forms such as circles, triangles, crosses, or bold lines. Color combinations are chosen in such a way that the two adjacent colors contrast with each other as well as with the environment in order to achieve maximum recognizability.

Applied colors should create safe work conditions without a decrease in productivity.

For example, the color yellow makes elements more visible; red indicates danger; and light green reduces fatigue in the human eye. According to its function, each element is colored entirely or partially. For example, while loose elements are colored in yellow, their ends (as the most dangerous part) are colored in red. Special artificial colors such as "safety green" (to mark voltage) are chosen due to their visibility and used at places where objects should be recognized from far away. The visual spectrum that lies between green and yellow has the most visible wavelength: 555 nm.[1] Initially, this currently fashionable color was invented for the ultimately practical purpose of visibility. Color is a tool of communication with the user.

It is another way to transmit information about a particular element or an entire structure. Depending on its purpose, this communication can be either very descriptive or discreet, but in any case, it is built on the rules of communication. And this rational technical language creates its utilitarian poetry, functional ornament. Contradistinguishing itself against the name of the famous essay by Adolf Loos, "Ornament and Crime," tecture acclaims: Ornament is prime!

The application of safety elements has its own rules and does not take any consideration of the building's tectonics. Safety tecture exists in its own parallel reality.

In the same way these elements ignore the architectural concept, architects almost always completely ignore them too. In most cases, architects create their dramatic spatial compositions genuinely along similar principles as in the *Ideal City* painting of an unknown artist from Central Italy, even though it is clear from the beginning that their design will be transformed by safety requirements later.

"Temporary" does not always equal "lightweight" or "transparent." Temporary windowless passages made of concrete and steel are not questioned by the public or labeled an obstacle due to their theoretical ephemerality. Ironically, some construction sites go on for years and surpass the lifespan of architecture in the conventional sense.

The superiority of safety is undoubtedly stronger than all other notions in any culture that the visual expression reaches to its extreme. Boldness and radicality are the results—no matter how visually disturbing the impact is. If designed architecture includes such topics as safety regulations as a matter of inspiration (along with spatial experience and speculative concept), the design could attempt far more radical, functional, and formally innovative solutions.

1   Cecie Starr, *Biology: Concepts and Applications* (Thomson Brooks/Cole, 2005), 94.

Hanging on a crane, the shield protects the surrounding buildings and streets from the debris and loose pieces that can fall during the demolition.

Construction site shield, Basel, Switzerland

Railway safety equipment, Lausanne, Switzerland

One can be surprised to see multiple brooms along railway tracks: what is their purpose? Art installations or cleaning equipment? In fact, these brushes are part of safety regulations and alert train drivers of protruding elements.

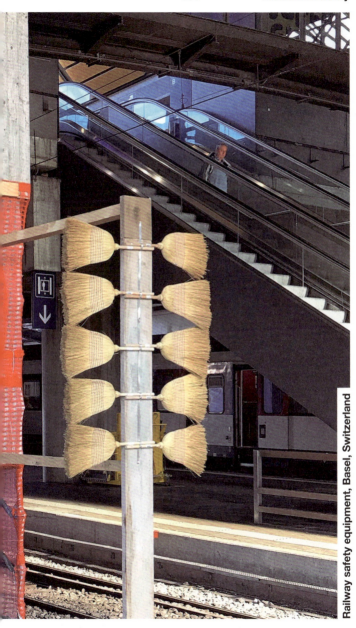

Railway safety equipment, Basel, Switzerland

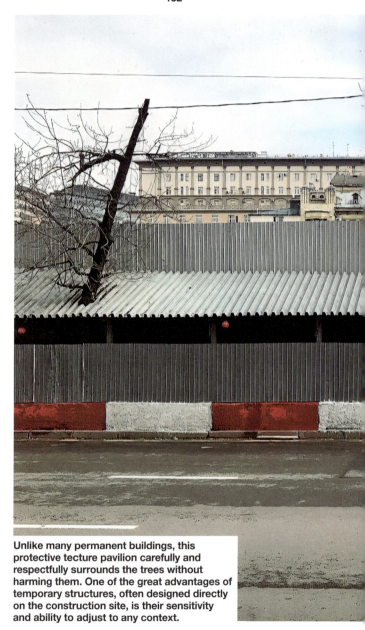

Unlike many permanent buildings, this protective tecture pavilion carefully and respectfully surrounds the trees without harming them. One of the great advantages of temporary structures, often designed directly on the construction site, is their sensitivity and ability to adjust to any context.

Temporary walkways near a construction site, Moscow, Russia

Foam rubber tubes protect pedestrians in Madrid, Spain

Tecture for tecture: these elements protect people from being hurt by structures and protect structures from being damaged or dismantled by people.

Wrapped scaffold pole, Geneva, Switzerland

Wrapped *Bauprofile* poles, Zurich, Switzerland

Mini fire station, Giardini during the Biennale, Venice, Italy

Foam rubber tubes protection, Venice, Italy

Triangle to prevent parking, Moscow, Russia

Diverse requirements create unique hybrid design: here, a "No Parking" pole needs to be visible, therefore it is colored with red and white stripes; it should move, therefore it is foldable; it has to withstand wind loads, therefore it has a suspended hanging stone.

Pole to prevent parking, Geneva, Switzerland

Painted floor marking temporary vehicle exit in Nice, France

Movable block to prevent parking, Moscow, Russia

Safety band outlining the potential danger, Brasilia, Brazil

Ladders on a construction site facade to demarcate the edges of open slabs, prevent falling, and provide additional means for fixation.

Construction of a new building, Barcelona, Spain

Color combinations are functional and alert of danger in the most efficient manner, creating their own bold and inspiring visual language.

Underpass under scaffolding in Geneva, Switzerland

Walkway sheds in Turin, Italy

Colors contrast with each other as well as with the environment. These combinations differ from city to city, creating distinct identities for urban spaces.

Walkway shed in Interlaken, Switzerland

Walkway shed in Moscow, Russia

"Temporary" isn't always equal "lightweight" or "transparent." Windowless passages built for disassembly from concrete blocks and steel can support the loads of construction cranes.

Walkway shed in Basel, Switzerland

Walkway protection, Sydney, Australia

Some construction sites last longer than permanent architecture, giving temporary solutions a permanent significance.

Walkway shed in Moscow, Russia

The presence of safety tecture
in the city is not questioned by
the public or labeled an obstacle
as their temporal ephemerality
outweighs their physical brutality.

Drying floor paint on the street in Geneva, Switzerland

Safety elements create their own rules and urban fluxes. Their universal language is recognized and understood globally, yet it is rarely acknowledged as an essential layer of the built environment.

Unique architectural patterns are created by following simple rules and rational logics. Here, "Do Not Cross" plastic band is wrapped around poles to mark the danger.

Scaffolding canopy in Biel, Switzerland

Event

Empire Stadium ski jump, Vancouver, Canada

Event structures pop up where events or temporary action take place. Their main purpose is to provide facilities: a concert stage at ancient ruins, a ski jump in a historical city square, or a bridge across a wild river. Event facilities create super-temporary architecture with exaggerated monofunctionality. They add function to a symbol, which creates its iconic appearance.

Event structures operate with traditional architectural notions—function, structure, and beauty—but all of them are treated as a separate layer and applied on top of one another independently due to their temporariness. There are functional elements, structural elements, and elements of beauty. Division of these elements is absolutely clear and logical.

Functionality is achieved by the appropriate material in its minimal amount placed on top of the structure. Be it a sliding surface of a ski jump, a tent protecting a stage from sun and rain, or a walking surface of a temporary bridge, the functionality is brought to its extreme in its physical representation.

Structural elements use as little material as possible to provide enough structural strength. Their only purpose is to take the load, so meanings of beauty or additional functionality never apply to them.

Elements of beauty—most often represented by print on a textile or banner fabric—are applied on top as a thin independent layer. Beauty can easily be removed or adjusted without affecting the functionality and stability of the structure, depending on the meaning of the event.

It is interesting to see how honest these structures are: decoration is clearly decoration, function is only function, and minimal structure is almost invisible due to its absolute rationality and economic efficiency.

Architects could probably learn to bring the purpose of each element to its absolute and find harmony in their coexistence, rather than bringing all the elements to the same old formula of function-structure-beauty.

The Kumbh Mela celebration in India is the largest gathering of people in the contemporary world. Every twelve years, approximately 100 million visitors travel for the ceremony of a holy dip at Sangam—the meeting point of the muddy waters of the Ganges and the bright-green waters of the Yamuna rivers. To take millions of pedestrians across the river, twenty-two temporary bridges are erected. The bridge structures consist of more than 1,700 steel pontoons and ensure transfer of an unthinkable quantity of people equal to several European countries in a very short period of time.[1]

Sport events are a unique mode, when a context has to be transformed drastically in order to host enormous but temporary action. Tecture is often a tool for efficient spatial transformations which are in such a demand in the sports industry. One of the first large-scale ski jumps was erected at Soldier

Field, Chicago, in 1936.[2] The temporary timber construction reached its highest point at 60 meters. The structure was built ultimately for practical purposes. The brilliance of the construction technologies demonstrated in this 60-meter wood ramp makes it a much more remarkable spatial statement than any designed-to-impress architectural exercise.

Public events are usually massive in scale and have a very short time span, considerably shorter even than the construction for these events. Therefore, the size and life-span of tecture for events is proportionate to the events and is particularly impressive and radical.

1 Inderjit Bhadwar, "Kumbh Mela: Nectar of the Gods," *India Today*, May 15, 1986.
2 Eben Lehman, "When Timber Engineers Brought Ski Jumping to Chicago," *Peeling Back the Bark*, October 7, 2009, https://fhsarchives.wordpress.com/2009/10/07/chicago-ski-jumping/.

Winegrower's Festival, Vevey, Switzerland, August 1955

Seamingly scaleless huge structures are actually designed with respect to human scale: the weight of the elements allows workers to carry each of them by hands. Ski jumps appear all around the world and are completely detached from the season or mountain location: they can appear in a city center in summer or on a lake shore in spring.

★ SPONSORED BY CO & G.

Empire Stadium ski jump, Vancouver, Canada

SPONSORED BY COW & GATE

Crowd control barriers, Barcelona, Spain

Ski jump, Moscow, Russia

The Star Performing Arts Centre, Singapore

Seating has been carefully marked in public areas to promote safe distancing in Singapore.

Pontoon bridges built for Maha Kumbh Mela festival, Allahabad, India

Protection

Shop window covers are torn down during protests, Paris, France

Protection is any action taken to prevent or minimize potential damage caused by an external force. One of the most important parameters of protection is efficiency. This parameter in architecture is based on availability of resources. How quickly and efficiently architecture can be protected with accessible construction material by the available workforce defines the success of protective measures. When there is no time, resources, or apparent necessity for permanent means of protection, temporary solutions are used.

Methods of protecting architecture are fairly diverse, ranging from camouflaging objects to make them invisible to an enemy to securing their structural strength to protect them from harmful physical contact. The chosen solution is often defined by the scale of the object that is to be protected, the type of danger, and "resolution" of a matter of protection. The area of protection varies from urban districts or even cities to small decorative details or single standing monuments. In any case, the parameter of efficiency in protective solutions fully dominates any other aspect. In combination with nontrivial tasks, it forces protective tecture to be innovative.

War is one of the greatest disasters in the world, ruining, along with human lives, nature, cities, and architecture. Tecture is often a solution to help saving architectural monuments, and to protect and fix urban infrastructure or defend private property.

During the First World War, in France sandbag structures were used to protect architectural monuments in the areas of intensive military actions. Cheap, fast, and easy to build and disassemble, made out of ubiquitous material, temporary reinforcement with sandbags helped preserve important bystanders of history. It is noteworthy that the same sandbags used to protect architecture were also used to protect French soldiers in their trenches. Piles of bags filled with sand and earth formed the defense system of Notre-Dame d'Amiens in Amiens, France; 10-meter-tall temporary structures protected the walls of the cathedral both inside and outside.

Almost a century later, in 2022, many monuments in Ukraine were covered by sandbags in preparation for the attacks of Russia's military forces. Cheap and easy to assemble, sandbag cocoons enveloped many self-standing monuments in historical squares in the city of Odessa and other cities. Sandbag structures appear not only in areas of military conflicts, but are actively used in case of floods, fires, and earthquakes. It is indicative that the same technical solution is used to protect people, houses, settlements, and territories from natural and anthropogenic hazards.

During the Second World War, Moscow urgently needed to protect itself against enemy bombing. A special department was formed with architects and artists to disguise the most important facilities, such as defense plants, water stations, the Kremlin, the Central Telegraph, oil storage, and city bridges. This project consisted of several measures: repainting the roofs and open facades of the Kremlin buildings to create a false perspective image, which would confuse enemy pilots and prevent them from finding strategically important objects to bomb. Kremlin stars were hidden by wooden panels, and the golden domes were disguised as well.

To disorient the enemy, fake city blocks were constructed in large open areas. On top of Lenin's Mausoleum in the Red Square, there was a plywood model of a generic building. Some streets were covered with plywood roofs, whereas wastelands were built up as fake factories with artificial light.

Tecture protects not only buildings from the impact of people, but people from the dangerous processes that happen inside the buildings. One of such cases is fumigation, a procedure of disinfecting a structure or a house from harmful microorganisms or insects by filling the volume of the structure with gaseous pesticides. This method requires complete isolation of the volume of the disinfected area to protect neighboring areas from the poison and to process fumigation efficiently. Temporary structures are the most efficient tool to create alternative climatic conditions around the treated volume and to protect people and the environment in a quick and a efficient manner. Fumigating tecture is a colorful tent wrapped around the existing structure. Contrasting patterns and bright colors announce the toxicity and danger, similar to dangerous species of animals. At the same time, they remind us of the traveling Chapiteau circus and emphasize the temporality of the structure.

During the protests of the *gilets jaunes* (yellow vests) in France in 2018, around 125,000 protesters took to the streets to oppose new fuel taxes introduced by Emmanuel Macron's government.[1] Paris was the epicenter of the protests, and here the most dramatic violence happened. Besides the police and the government, the subject of protesters' anger included banks, boutiques, luxury shops, restaurants, and corporate offices. The ground floors of those buildings, especially their windows, were the easiest targets for vandalization and destruction. The windows represented the power of capitalism, and many were burned or broken. In order to protect shops, many owners boarded up their windows with plywood, corrugated metal, or gypsum board panels.

These examples show how tecture can adjust and transform space at a high speed and with unique efficiency. Digitalization of our life increases the speed of change required by the physical environment, and architecture in particular. Tecture keeps up with the speed of these changes much easier than traditional architecture. To a certain point, temporary structures serve as a connector between the requirements of the digital world and the possibilities of the analog realities.

1 "France Protests: PM Philippe Suspends Fuel Tax Rises," *BBC News*, December 4, 2018, https://www.bbc.com/news/world-europe-46437904.

1111118

Protection of the Notre-Dame d'Amiens cathedral with sandbags, Amiens, France, 1940–1945

During the Second World War, the historical monuments were covered with temporary wooden pavilions to prevent the damage. Their design, following purely rational logic, is strikingly modern and contradicts the conserved historical image of St. Petersburg.

Camouflaged Monument to Nicholas I, St. Petersburg, Russia, 1943–1944

Construction of a brick dome to protect Michelangelo's Statue of David during the Second World War, Florence, Italy, 1943

Michelangelo's Statue of David. Constructed brick dome, Florence, Italy, 1943

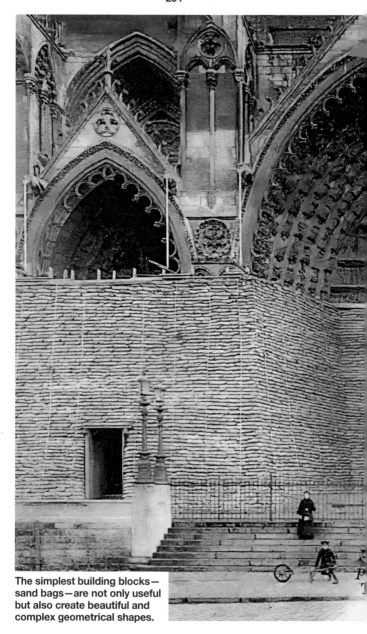

The simplest building blocks—
sand bags—are not only useful
but also create beautiful and
complex geometrical shapes.

NS (Somme) - **La Cathédrale** ~ *Le Grar
par des sacs de sable, contre l'incursion des
thedral - The gread doovs protected by bags
against the taubes*

Sandbags protecting the Notre-Dame d'Amiens cathedral in Amiens, France, in the First World War.

Just a layer of paint was the most efficient and cheap way of completely transforming huge historical buildings. Those trompe l'oeils gave a misleading image of the buildings from the air and prevented bombing.

Red Army Theater, Moscow, Russia, 1941

Moscow Manége painted as residential buildings, Moscow, Russia, 1941

Lockheed Aircraft's camouflaged factory in Burbank, California, USA

A fake city was built next to the Boeing factory in the USA in order to disorient the enemy during potential aerial attacks.

Fake residential buildings next to the Boeing factory, Seattle, Washington, USA, 1942

Monument to Princess Olga, the Apostle Andrew, St. Cyril and
St. Methodius, protected by sandbags. Kyiv, Ukraine, March 2022

Most luxury brands were the primary targets of the protesters' vandalism. Tecture to cover the windows was rapidly created from the cheapest and most accessible local materials.

Boarded shop windows during the Yellow Vests protests, Paris, France

It created a strong visual contradiction with the lavish decorative facades made of expensive materials such as carved stone porticoes, huge glass panes, and brass window frames.

Boarded shop windows during protests, Paris, France

Cheap plywood versus a decorative neoclassical stone facade: direct coexistence of architecture and tecture, where tecture is the one that copes with an urgent social problem.

Boarded shop windows during protests, Paris, France

Pattern of protection and accessible materials: masking tape and wooden fiber board.

Boarded shop windows during protests, Paris, France

Pretending to be invisible: tecture helps a lavishly decorated boutique shop window to disappear.

Boarded shop windows during protests, Paris, France

Protesters remove protections on shop windows in Paris, France

Protective metall wall to cover the ongoing construction, Brussels, Belgium

Tecture communicates through color about the extremely dangerous conditions inside.

Fumigation of a private house, Pelham, Alabama, USA

Vernacular

Traditional bamboo scaffolding covering a generic modern high-rise building in Hong Kong, China

By definition, vernacular is architecture concerned with domestic and functional buildings. Its etymological origin comes from the Latin word *vernaculus* (domestic, native, from *verna*, home-born slave). The home-born slave is a fitting metaphor for such structures and utilitarian architecture in general. It shows how it is tied to a specific place, its servile function, its anonymity, and its hardworking purpose.

Tecture is urban vernacular architecture, which, in response to specific needs, contributes to the life and image of the city. It reflects cultural standards, social norms, and the availability of materials. Today, the local specificity of architecture has gained a new level of importance. Environmental challenges force us to revisit the logic of resource availability and the traditions of coping with local climates in an efficient and sustainable way. The industrialization of architecture, globalization of the construction industry, and internationally shared cultural and aesthetic standards of design make us lose locally developed methods of construction.

Industrially produced architecture in a particular city often does not define or reflect local specificities: a generic Miesian skyscraper or a signature masterpiece by any international architectural practice can appear in any national, social, climatic, or political context. This happens because the character of designed architecture comes from the current style and personal tastes of architects or their clients, the allocated budget for construction, and the organization of the industry, which makes shipping industrially produced materials from another part of the world cheaper than local production. The acceleration of construction speed requires prefabricated, easy-to-assemble solutions, leading to a loss of expertise in working with non-clip-in solutions. Often, local specificity is reflected through the ornamentalization of the building or the use of materials conventionally recognized as traditional for decoration. However, the actual responsible consumption of resources and the specificity of the climate are rarely truly addressed by design solutions and methods of construction.

One of the essential purposes of architecture is to provide the required functionality using available resources. Tecture in these terms embodies the essence of architecture. Despite the rotation of architectural narratives and focus of professional discourse, tecture has always maintained a direct connection with the context in which it was erected. Technologies used for tecture follow the same goal as traditional vernacular knowledge: to create the cheapest, most-efficient, and fast-to-produce solutions by local master builders. Traditional local vernacular materials have become exotic luxuries, or historical pastiche in many cases, while the actual place of vernacular architecture around the world is taken by tecture.

In our opinion, contemporary vernacular architecture does not always mean constructed out of local materials, but rather constructed out of locally available materials to address the particularities of context and climatic conditions. Tecture is not ultimately vernacular construction, but it demonstrates the logic of vernacular architecture in its details and method of construction. It employs low-tech, almost-primitive construction solutions to cope with the challenges of the context, demonstrating how simple and efficient responses to low temperatures, wind loads, aggressive sun, and heat can be.

Tecture, which appears anonymously, out of necessity, and according to local regulations and conditions, is not restricted by the aesthetic preference of clients or romanticized historical references. Its logic is determined by purely rational reasons: structural stability, climatic specificities of the region, available building materials, local security, and reasonable health regulations. All of these factors mentioned above allow tecture, to a certain extent, to be described as the new urban vernacular.

Bamboo scaffolding is used mostly in Southeast Asia and India. It is the ideal material for tecture: lightweight, easily accessible, cheap, 100-percent recyclable, and renewable, and therefore ecological.

Building under construction, Hong Kong, China

Traditional bamboo scaffolding is often used in the context of loose application of construction security requirements.

Bamboo scaffolding, Hong Kong, China

Exceptionally elaborate vernacular bamboo scaffolding and fabric "cocoons" showcase examples of handmade artisanal architecture. Ironically, often they facilitate the creation of generic and rather banal skyscrapers.

Building under construction, Hong Kong, China

Building under construction, Hong Kong, China

Pragmatic reuse of local textiles
transforms a construction site into an
ornamental patchwork art piece.

Building under construction, Dakar, Senegal

Bauprofile (or *Gabarit* in French) is
a typical Swiss typology of tecture. It
is a space holder for a building, which
indicates the reserved space for
a future construction and allows the
people (usually neighbors) to directly
influence the architectural project by
voting for or against it. A beautiful
concept, "invisible future buildings
from air", they are actually purely
pragmatic.

Bauprofile, Basel, Switzerland

Bauprofile, Regensdorf, Switzerland

Flexibility of bamboo allows it to follow complex curved shapes.

Pagoda dome under renovation, Bagan, Myanmar

Rather primitive technology and simple, cheap materials create intricate laces of shadow and light. Such "cocoons" could be easily imagined as permanent solutions to prevent overheating.

Building under construction, Istanbul, Turkey

Insulating the construction site in winter gives a soft, but radically monumental appearance to a traditional house.

Insulation of a construction site in winter, Russia

New Order

Restoration of the Colosseum, Rome, Italy

In the treatise *Essay on Architecture*, Marc-Antoine Laugier suggests that the appearance and architectonic characteristics of ancient Greek temples were predefined by early proto-buildings: primitive huts. Trunks of trees dug in the ground served as columns to support massive horizontal wood beams, on which the simplest roof rested to protect from rainwater and sun. Gaps between structural elements were covered by vertical wood planks. Practical logic and basic structural principles were later developed in the Doric order. This set of rules has been decorated and beautified many times and determined the development of Western architecture for centuries to come. Ironically, the highly technological engineering invention of ancient days was studied by architects primarily from an aesthetic point of view. The beauty of an utilitarian wooden structure was adopted and transferred to stone, then to concrete, and even steel architecture, without big adjustments to the structural qualities of the new materials, often disregarding their physical potential. Technical solutions born out of practicality, availability of the material, construction technologies, and economy were conserved in a system of aesthetical cannons and defined by the law of architecture (order).

In contrast and throughout its history, tecture has been free from aesthetic judgments, political ambitions, tastes of clients, styles, and fashions, yet always controlled by budget limitations and technologies. That freedom on one side (from aesthetics and politics) and restrictions on the other (from technology and budget) resulted in a set of rules, concepts, and qualities that exist in a parallel reality to designed architecture. The same way in which purely rational structural logic was originally a base for the classical order of architecture, tecture has created a new order, which has never been manifested so far due to the absence of an author.

What can we as architects learn from tecture's new order, and why should we look at it? Contemporary architecture tries to be novel: radical, unique, ecologically responsible, contextual—and immediately becomes obsolete. Tecture does not try to be anything of the above, but eventually gets to be all of it. It happens because it exists in a different aesthetic dimension—of contemporary engineering. It uses the achievements of contemporary technology without super complex and expensive solutions (like in high-tech engineering) and without romanticizing it in post-reflections of the author (like in high-tech architecture, for instance). Tecture is the temporary structure for everyday life, and it achieves maximum efficiency with minimum means. Tecture combines the technological achievements with the smart and economical use of resources.

Probably this approach—a well-balanced position between simplicity and technology, cost-efficiency and functionality—could be learned by contemporary architecture from temporary structures. Structures that at each step follow the logic of practicality happen to be simultaneously innovative, beautiful, functional, and ecological. These types of structures do not age, while the function they serve is in demand and context does not undergo massive transformations. They cannot be judged aesthetically if functionality is the essence of the object. Almost through its entire history, architecture simply appropriated and beautified practical innovations. Perhaps orientation on functional innovation is a promising direction of architectural development. Classical architectural order was denoted by ancient utilitarian structures, which gives us the right to suggest that the new order of contemporary architecture could be declared by utilitarian structures of our current time.

The new order of tecture, which has never been manifested, has its main inherent qualities, analogous to the Vitruvian triad of strength, utility, and beauty. We believe that the new order triad following the contemporary challenges has mutually developed to be:

essential
efficient
honest

essential

ARCHITECTS SHOULD TRY NOT TO BUILD

As tecture appears only where it is absolutely necessary, architecture should be erected when there is no other possibility to achieve the set goals. We have to minimize spatial transformation but develop the management of space in time. Each single physical element proposed by the architect is a consumption of resources today and the generation of waste in the future. It does not mean construction has to be absolutely banned, but it requires a deep analysis of all the possible alternatives to minimize new physical interventions. The architect is in charge of the transformation of the space, but the necessity of spatial intervention should be carefully evaluated each time.

REGIME OF USE 24/7: DENSITY OF HOURS OF USE INSTEAD OF SQUARE METERS

Architects should intensify hours of the use of the buildings rather than increase the amount of the built area. The more processes we can accommodate in the same building, the better for the environment. We have to find a way to share different processes in the same space in the same time, so each square meter is used 24 hours a day, 7 days a week.

Architects should shift from the role of chief builders to the role of chief curators of the space, materials, and resources on time.

efficient

MAXIMUM EFFECT WITH MINIMUM MEANS
We live in the context of increasing scarcity of resources, and in future, this problem will only escalate. Architecture should try to reach its goals with the most efficient solutions. This always requires conscientious and minimal use of building materials. The latest technologies should be used yet without worshipping them. Sometimes low-tech buildings appear to be more contemporary, robust, and technologically relevant. Basic but smart solutions age more slowly than highly technological but very specific ones. The reuse and further development of elementary solutions are significantly easier than working with outdated high-tech elements, which sometimes can only be replaced.

REUSE AND FLEXIBILITY
Tecture reuses the same elements and materials for new purposes, and they appear reassembled in new places. That is crucial for sustainable architecture and allows programmatic flexibility and circularity in construction. Architecture should be designed to live many lives, both in terms of materials and in terms of program. Contemporary buildings should be designed for disassembly and reassembly: partially or entirely, possibly at a new location, for another user and another program.

honest

NAKED PURPOSE

Design should be brave and honest. Each element in a building should announce its actual purpose and structure. It should not be ashamed to reveal the number of layers in the wall build-up, the artificiality of the material, and the decorative purpose of other elements. The design has to reveal and underline the quality of each material and the purpose of each element. Design built on the significance of actual qualities is more explicit, innovative, and conceptually strong.

All that does not mean that architecture should evolve into purely utilitarian construction, ignoring urban context and human feelings. Beauty is also one of the functions of a building. Similarly, consideration of the context is an important part of any design. Yet beauty and context should be an inherent part of the design, tightly connected to its function and purpose.

COLOR AND DETAILS AS UNIVERSAL COMMUNICATION TOOLS

Colors and details can transmit most information about function, scale, safety requirements, and navigation throughout a building. When these elements are used as tools of communication, they create enough visual expression and do not require any additional designed beautification.

Tecture does not seek out its aesthetics; instead it declares them, stating: this type of technology or function looks like that. If you need this exact function, you have to accept this appearance.

Contributions

Time is the essential fourth parameter in a three-dimensional attempt to define spatial conditions. Temporality in architecture holds a central position in many reflections on the organization of the built environment. "Architecture does not pass in time; time passes in architecture," states Bob van Reeth succinctly on the determinative role of time in architecture. The more we reflected on the inevitability of temporal change, the more pressing the question became: How permanent should our solutions be?

Three very different authors who investigate, through their practice, the availability of resources and their utilization over time as key aspects of the process of creating the built environment have been invited to contribute to this book.

This invitation was driven by our desire to add another perspective to the topic, creating a more stereoscopic view. To reflect on the phenomenon of contemporary temporary utilitarian structures at the intersection of architectural practice, research, and history, we invited three prominent authors from these three respective fields: practicing architect Jan De Vylder, architectural historian and theorist Philip Ursprung, and Charlotte Malterre-Barthes, who, besides being an architect and theorist, is also well known for her strong activist position.

Holding It Together: The Architecture of Scaffolding

by Charlotte Malterre-Barthes

"Scaffold: from Anglo-Norman French, from Old French (e)*schaffaut*, from the base of catafalque, a decorated wooden framework supporting the coffin of a distinguished person during a funeral or while lying in state.
- a temporary structure on the outside of a building, made of wooden planks and metal poles, used by workers while building, repairing, or cleaning the building
- the materials used in scaffolding. 'a truck carrying scaffolding'
- a raised wooden platform used formerly for the public execution of criminals."[1]

In the distance, set against the Parisian gray sky, a futuristic structure made of intricate metal rods emerges. On second glance, there is not much futuristic about it—quite the opposite: it is the colossal scaffolding that outlines the to-be-reconstructed structure of Notre Dame de Paris, badly damaged by a massive fire in 2019. Partly dedicated to rebuilding the 100-meter spire, a 600-ton metal structure towers over the remains of the historical building (fig. 1). But before it could be installed, a 200-ton scaffolding had to be removed, the one put in place to renovate the spire before the fire. Some 40,000 pieces of tangled, mangled steel rods had been melted and deformed by the blaze. A lightweight scaffolding was erected around the old one to allow skilled workers to take this metallic mess apart and away (fig. 2).[2] A phantom fourth scaffolding was present, albeit only in the archive, a wood one designed by Eugène Viollet-le-Duc to rebuild the spire demolished during the Revolution, part of the overall effort to renovate the whole cathedral in 1857 (fig. 3).[3] These four scaffoldings of Notre Dame de Paris, interwoven through space and time, exemplify how what is often perceived as a temporary and unremarkable aspect of construction reveals more than its structural role: namely the history of technology and machines, norms, labor practices, and economic growth while also operating as a commentary on how society cares for its built environment.

While a comprehensive history of architectural scaffolding is yet to be written, architecture historians have partially tackled the topic. Stefan Holzer and Nicoletta Marconi researched the creative scaffolding practice of Saint Peter's *Fabbrica* at the Vatican and of scaffold master Nicola Zabaglia, ultimately unfolding a history of the development of the technology of fixed and mobile scaffolding in construction and restoration practices across Europe.[4] It is also part of the renovation of Notre Dame de Paris in 1857, after the cathedral narrowly avoided demolition, that while overseeing the reconstruction site Viollet-le-Duc designed the adapted scaffolding, a task considered to be one for a carpenter.[5] Scaffolding has a long history, with bamboo structures depicted in Chinese art around 1000, for instance, in *Along the River During the Qingming Festival*, a piece by imperial artist Zhang Zeduan (1085–1145). Bamboo and wood still prevail in many countries and have not yet been supplanted by metal due to availability, sturdiness, affordability, and expertise. In the Western world, scaffolding mirrors the history of modernity and technology. At the advent of the Industrial Revolution, iron and steel became more readily available, and metal tubes and fittings saw the emergence of standardized scaffolding systems made with aluminum and other lightweight materials. Modern scaffolding now incorporates frame scaffolds, tube and clamp techniques, and safety gear on the structures, including nets, harnesses, and guardrails. Safety regulations, material standards, and load-bearing requirements by insurance and public authorities mean standardization is the norm, although customized scaffolding can be produced for specific projects and conditions. Yet scaffolding remains a marginal topic within architecture; its design and installation heavily standardized and not considered to be the task of an architect.

Scaffolding stands at the intersection of public and private spaces and often encroaches onto streets and sidewalks, disrupting pedestrian flows and road traffic. While public safety is the primary motivation behind regulating this construction site spillover, it is workers operating on scaffolding, moving at dangerous heights with minimal protection, who are the most at risk. The Occupational Safety and Health Administration (OSHA) in the United States has detailed standards for scaffold construction, including requirements for strength, structural integrity, and accessibility.[6] The Swiss Engineers and Architects group (SIA) regulates scaffolding with the norm "SIA 118/222—Allgemeine

Bedingungen für Gerüstbau/General Terms and Conditions for Scaffolding."[7] Even if safety regulations insist on rigorous standards, including high-grade materials, mandatory safety harnesses, guardrails, and stable platforms, scaffolding accidents remain the second leading cause of injuries on construction sites. In addition, accidents have increased by about 800 percent over the last five years, a growth attributable to the construction sector's constant increase.[8] Aggregated research shows that lack of guardrails, "edge protection," working at night, and improper assembly of scaffolding are responsible. This rather gloomy outline has not impacted the industry itself.

A scaffold costs about 10 to 20 euros per square meter, with costs increasing with height due to wind and risk, to which a daily rental fee must be added. Costs vary widely across countries and are adjusted based on soil resistance, complexity of the project, and many other factors. Considering that the scaffolding industry is part of the construction sector, it should come as no surprise that it is doing well economically, with a global market value of USD 55 billion and an expected increase of 6 percent annually.[9]

If scaffolding conceptually seems like a sort of accommodating twin to architecture—materializing the logistics necessary to tackle the construction or maintenance of buildings (from the outside in or, when installed inside, from the inside out), as a helpful structure—it is also a stark reminder that architects design but, as Nicoleta Marconi pointed out, "it is the builders who make the structure real."[10]

While scaffolding is little considered in design processes and is expected to adjust to serve the construction of the project, in society and the realm of metaphors, *scaffolding* as a term enjoys conceptual popularity.[11] It represents support, growth, and the transitory nature of development. As an underlying framework that facilitates the realization of grander visions, the metaphor extends to social constructs, where scaffolding symbolizes support systems to uplift individuals and communities. In psychology, scholars have investigated the origin of the term as a "temporary adaptive support" and wondered why it emerged. They trace it to Russian constructivism: "To understand the Soviet connotations of this metaphor in the revolutionary texts, one needs to be aware that everything was under construction at that time and constructivist metaphors mostly meant strong determinacy of the future by current efforts based on socialist politics."[12]

If, in psychology, the scaffolding metaphor speaks to the possibility and facilitation of accomplishing a task and bridging the present to an anticipated future state, culturally, the actual physical presence of scaffolding signals change and renewal. It may also bring a sense of dread and temporariness, particularly regarding the maintenance of existing buildings. After two buildings collapsed in 2018 in the center of Marseille, a tragedy caused by bad governance and lack of upkeep, scaffolding appeared all over the affected district of Noailles.[13] Translating the fear of structural instability, scaffolding became a visual metaphor of neglect and decay, especially when it remained longer than it should have. Yet scaffolding as helpful structures that draw attention to our existing stock of building hold much potential, particularly as care and repair are topics that have gained popularity in the architecture discourse of late.[14] These are not new; feminist artists and heritage and preservation specialists have worked on them for decades.[15] Yet this emerging trend could bring maintenance to the forefront of architecture, a task typically considered outside of the discipline's scope, with architects' interest in scaffolding and its design potential increasing—the present book a possible forecast for this shift.

Fig. 1 Scaffolding of Notre Dame, December 2023.

Fig. 2 Removal of the previous scaffolding and the new lightweight structure, Notre Dame, July 2020, *le Parisien.*

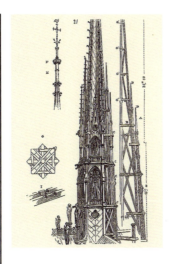

Fig. 3   Élévation et plans de la flèche de Notre-Dame de Paris par Viollet-le-Duc, in: Eugène Viollet-le-Duc, *Dictionnaire raisonné de l'architecture française du XIe au XVIe siècle*, 1866.

1   Michael Marks, *Scaffolding: The Handbook for Estimating and Product Knowledge* (Page Publishing, Incorporated, 2016), 9.

2   Pauline Conradson, "Notre-Dame: où en est le chantier titanesque?," *Le Parisien*, July 9, 2020, https://www.leparisien.fr/culture-loisirs/notre-dame-de-paris-ou-en-est-le-chantier-titanesque-09-07-2020-8350419.php.

3   Eugène-Emmanuel Viollet-le-Duc, *Dictionnaire raisonne de l'architecture française du XIe au XVIe siecle* (Paris: B. Bance, A. Morel, 1858), vol. 5, 459.

4   Stefan M. Holzer and Nicoletta Marconi, "Nicola Zabaglia's Scaffoldings for the Maintenance of Architectural Space in St. Peter's Basilica and Throughout Europe in the Seventeenth to Nineteenth Centuries," in *Creating Place in Early Modern European Architecture*, ed. Elizabeth Merrill (Amsterdam: Amsterdam University Press, 2022).

5   See Laurence de Finance, Jean-Michel Leniaud, and Cité de l'architecture et du patrimoine, *Viollet-Le-Duc: les visions d'un architecte* (Paris: Cité de l'architecture & du patrimoine, Norma Éditions Paris, 2014).

6   "Scaffolding," *Occupational Safety and Health Administration*, https://www.osha.gov/scaffolding, accessed April 18, 2024.

7   "Allgemeine Bedingungen Für Gerüstbau," in SIA 118/222:2012 (Zurich: SIA, 2012), 11.

8   AbdulLateef Olanrewaju, Jack Son Khor, and Christopher Nigel Preece, "An Investigation into Occupational Health and Safety of Scaffolding Practices on Construction Sites in Malaysia," in *Frontiers in Engineering and Built Environment* 2, no. 1 (2022), 3.

9   "Global Scaffolding Market to Reach $94.2 Billion by 2030," in *Global News Wire*, May 25, 2023, https://www.globenewswire.com/news-release/2023/05/25/2676456/0/en/Global-Scaffolding-Market-to-Reach-94-2-Billion-by-2030.html.

10   Holzer and Marconi, "Nicola Zabaglia's Scaffoldings," 238.

11   Zhe Yin and Carlos Caldas, "Scaffolding in Industrial Construction Projects: Current Practices, Issues, and Potential Solutions," *International Journal of Construction Management* 22, no. 13 (2022): 2554-2563.

12   Anna Shvarts and Arthur Bakker, "The Early History of the Scaffolding Metaphor: Bernstein, Luria, Vygotsky, and Before," *Mind, Culture, and Activity* 26, no. 1 (2019): 8.

13   See Marc Angélil and Charlotte Malterre-Barthes, and Something Fantastic, *Migrant Marseille. Architectures of Social Segregation and Urban Inclusivity* (Berlin: Ruby Press, 2020).

14   See Charlotte Malterre-Barthes and Dubravka Sekulić, "Curriculum Repair," ARCH+ *The Great Repair*, no. 250 (2023).

15   See Mierle Laderman Ukeles, "Manifesto for Maintenance Art 1969! Proposal for an Exhibition Care," *Journal of Contemporary Painting* 4, no. 2 (2018).

Parkhaus Oerlikon
by Jan De Vylder

Do we even know exactly what is going on here? We could know. By going to ask. But even if we don't go and ask. We could know. We can see it.

Something needs to be supported. That apparently doesn't work without some extra support. That extra support is needed. Otherwise it would not work. Not be able to work anymore.

Since when this is we do not know. Nor do we know how serious it is. Perhaps we can assume it wasn't right away. Something like this is not designed that way. Not right away anyway. Maybe we can assume it's not very serious either. It is certainly necessary. Yet it can still be assumed that other elements of the structural scheme of the building are sufficiently strong. For these additional elements cannot do it on their own. Certainly not the lateral movements. They are not even used for that.

Perhaps it could be suggested that the building once served a different purpose. But even that seems unlikely. The various ramps

Parkhaus Oerlikon with supporting scaffolding stilts that fix the structural problems of the building.

show that the building was designed for what it is today. A parking garage.

Moreover. There is an identical building a few blocks away. Also a parking garage. A virtually identical building. But without the additional support.

Perhaps one last possibility. Was there a problem with the ground surface? Or the foundation?

Then how would this help?

Now. Maybe enough assumptions. We could go and ask.

But we don't.

It's too interesting to not go and ask.

Just the assumptions above are enough to learn what architecture and structure may be about. The beautiful stacked rejuvenated columns tell it all: less needed above. And wider distribution below. Literalized theory. Materialized calculation. Structural aesthetics.

A lesson. And then another lesson.

Yellow. Why yellow? Why this yellow? A slightly strange and not exactly the prettiest yellow. But a very clear yellow. A signal yellow. A warning yellow. Safety. Visibility.

Don't counter. Never. And certainly not with this yellow. Lateral movement is

not the strong suit of this extra support.
At the same time. The support is not there
for that reason.

Oh well, maybe a little lateral strike won't
be such a drama after all.

But finally. And above all.

It is beautiful. This picture is beautiful.
This building is beautiful.

It tells the story of an architecture of
despair. It is not a question of what happened.
But a question of what was supposed to happen. And how that was answered. No demolitions. At least extensions. And probably for
longer than expected.

The longer this waits, the more the ques-
tions will be asked. Careless passers-by.
Amused architecture students. And engineers.
But also one-off and casual visitors parking.
Maybe even daily visitors. Maybe not even
those anymore. Why is this so?

Is there a café on the corner where they
tell the story? The story of despair?

Somehow this building tells the story
of what today is very much about: What
should we do with what we have? What can
we do with it? And how could it possibly be
done differently?

Beauty as a guide.

This essay was originally published
in Dutch in GLEAN (NL) magazine,
Volume 4, April 2024.

New Beginnings
by Philip Ursprung

What is it that makes ephemeral architecture appealing? Why are we attracted to temporary interventions? Why do provisional structures sometimes seem more relevant, more vital, more real than completed architecture?

In fall 2018, I went with my students to Georgia for a seminar week. During our stay in Tbilisi, we visited the Architecture Biennial. Unlike most other biennials, in which objects are displayed within exhibition spaces, the interventions happened in public spaces throughout the city. I was struck by an installation by Maria Kremer, entitled *Bridge-Habitat*. Kremer had inserted a wooden construction containing a small shopping mall into one of the arches of the DKD bridge, a pedestrian crossing from the Soviet era. From a distance, the wooden boards affixed to the concrete structure looked like a prosthetic supporting the bridge's partially decaying substance. Perhaps this is a safety measure, I thought, or the scaffolding for a new addition.

As I got closer to *Bridge-Habitat,* I noticed a wooden stairway leading to a timber construction under the concrete vault. I imagined what it would be like to live in this habitat, half-protected, half-exposed to the city. I recalled tree houses from my childhood and the *Cellules* that the artist/architect Absalon proposed to erect in public spaces in the 1990s. *Bridge-Habitat* was part of an architecture exhibition, but it was not a mock-up or a model. For me, the habitat acted like a lens. Suddenly, I saw the built environment clearer and could cherish its rawness and fragility. Rather than merely representing something, it did something.

Was *Bridge-Habitat* an emblem of the ambivalent situation of Georgia, a country in transition? Nestled in the ruins of the Soviet empire, it was simultaneously attached to and independent from its contours. It was a gesture of repair of a fragmented past. And it sketched out a future that has not yet found a definite form. No doubt, this intervention was site-specific to Tbilisi. And yet it also touched a more general issue that goes beyond the situation of Georgia, namely, the beauty of the temporary.

Temporary structures, scaffolding, and ephemeral elements attract us because they are beyond representation. They stand for what they are. They say: "Look, this is how it is. But it could also be different." They are performative, not static. They embody possibilities, processes, experiments. They inspire our imagination. They do not colonize spaces but produce them. They are by nature optimistic, constructive, forward-looking. There is nothing closed, defined, or tragic about them. They stand for ever new beginnings.

Conclusion

We as architects are dreaming and hoping to solve the problems and answer the challenges of the future. Yet, the tool that is used — architecture — is often too slow to cope with the challenges of the constantly changing present. Building construction takes too long and is too restricted by investment plans. Although one of the essential qualities of architecture is to grow and change, architecture is often seen as something complete, solid, and fixed, and architecture's definition outside of the profession — *Immobilien* (German for real estate), not movable — shows the attitude to architecture as an embodiment of private financial interest and not as a tool of societal improvement.

By the time a project is designed, all the permissions are received, and the structure is finally erected, reality has often changed so much that a newly completed building is already obsolete or has to undergo a renovation. As an answer to the quick pace of our changing world and the scarcity of resources, we see temporary architecture as a powerful and immediate tool that can actually allow us to dream, experiment, and really answer the pressing challenges of contemporary society. During recent events like the COVID-19 pandemic, the energy crisis, the wars in Ukraine and in the Middle East, the refugee crises, and others, temporary solutions proved most efficient in a state of emergency. Temporary architecture reaches the maximum effect with minimum means and is designed for constant reuse and recycling. Upcoming crises will require rethinking the meaning of *architecture* and the way we create it.

And what about aesthetics and beauty — if we are even allowed to talk about it in the academic context? Joseph Brodsky, a great poet and thinker, once wrote: "It is strange not to realize that beauty cannot be a goal, that it is always a by-product of other, often very mediocre pursuits."[1] That is the answer. And if the time of industrialization was represented by modernist architecture and later new technologies were represented by high-tech and digital architecture, we see temporary architecture as a representation of tomorrow: a rapidly changing society in a state of constant crisis.

1   Iosif Brodskij, *Fondamenta degli Incurabili*, tr. Gilberto Forti (Venice: Consorzio Venezia nuova, 1989), 26, 15.

Biographies

<u>KOSMOS Architects</u> is an experimental architectural practice that collaborates virtually across borders. The work of **KOSMOS** encompasses urban, architectural, and object design, as well as research and art installations, addressing environmental and social challenges. Through experimentation with materials and construction techniques, the practice explores the spatial and visual parameters of architecture to define its contemporary meaning at the intersection of material and immaterial realms. Leveraging expertise in diverse geographical contexts and projects of varying scales and types, along with a blend of practice and academic experience, KOSMOS explores opportunities for enhancing the built environment in cross-disciplinary fields.

KOSMOS was found by Artem Kitaev and Leonid Slonimskiy in 2012 as a design and research collaboration and transformed into an architectural practice in 2017.

<u>Jan De Vylder</u>, born 1968, is a Flemish architect based in Ghent and Brussels, Belgium. He has worked under his name since 2000. In 2005, together with Inge Vinck, jan de vylder architecten was founded. Later on, in 2010, architecten de vylder vinck taillieu was founded together with Inge Vinck and Jo Taillieu. And more recently, architecten jan de vylder inge vinck was founded with Inge Vinck. In these diverse constellations Jan De Vylder has realized several

works in Belgium and abroad and has been exhibited in galleries like MANIERA (BE), FRIEDMAN BENDA (US), TOTO MA (JP) and biennials (Venice 2010, 2014, 2016, 2018; Chicago 2014, 2016; Lisbon 2019; and Sao Paolo 2019). Since 2010 editing houses like 2G (ES), A+U (JP), deAedibus (CH), ARCHIVE (ES) and more recently TOTO Publishers (JP) have published several monographs on the work of Jan De Vylder. Moreover, he has won several international nominations and prizes, such as Schelling Architekturpreis 2016 (DE), Leone d'Argento at the Venice Biennale 2018 (IT), Henry van de Velde-award 2018 (BE); he was a nominated finalist for the Mies Award 2019 (EU). Jan De Vylder co-curated the Belgian Pavilion at the Venice Biennale in 2016. The exhibitions *Caroussel* 2015 (gta/ETH-Z); *Bravoure Scarcity Beauty* (Venice 2016) and *Unless Ever People* (Venice 2018) opened new reflections on architecture and practice. Jan De Vylder has taught at Sint-Lucas School for Architecture in Ghent and Brussels, at TU Delft, at EPFL Lausanne, and at Accademia di Architettura di Mendrisio. Since 2017 he has been teaching at ETH Zurich.

Charlotte Malterre-Barthes is an architect, urban designer, and assistant professor at the Swiss Federal Institute of Technology—EPFL, where she leads the laboratory RIOT. Most recently assistant professor at Harvard University, Malterre-Barthes's interests are related to urgent aspects of contemporary urbanization, material extraction, climate emergency, and ecological/social justice. In 2020 she started the initiative A Global Moratorium on New Construction, interrogating current development protocols (2025, Sternberg Press & MIT Press). A founding member of the Parity Group and of the Parity Front, activist networks dedicated to equality in architecture, Malterre-Barthes holds a PhD (ETH Zurich) on the political economy of commodities and the built environment.

Philip Ursprung studied art history, history and German language and literature in Geneva, Vienna, and Berlin and received his doctorate from the Freie Universität Berlin in 1993 and his habilitation from ETH Zurich in 1999.

He has taught at the HdK Berlin, Columbia University, Cornell University, the Barcelona Institute of Architecture and the Universities of Geneva and Basel. From 2005 to 2011, he was a professor of modern and contemporary art at the University of Zurich. Since 2011, he has been a professor of art and architectural history at ETH Zurich. From 2017 to 2019, he was head of the Department of Architecture. Since 2024, he has been head of the Institute for the History and Theory of Architecture. From 2015 to 2020, he led the research project "Tourism and Cultural Heritage" at the Future Cities Laboratory of the Singapore ETH Center in Singapore. He is editor of *Herzog & de Meuron: Natural History* (2002), co-editor of *Gordon Matta-Clark: An Archival Sourcebook* (2022) and others. Author of *Grenzen der Kunst: Allan Kaprow und das Happening, Robert Smithson und die Land Art* (Munich, 2003, English: 2013), *Die Kunst der Gegenwart: 1960 bis heute* (2010), *Der Wert der Oberfläche: Essays zu Kunst, Architektur und Ökonomie* (Zurich, 2017) and *Joseph Beuys: Kunst, Kapital, Revolution* (2021). In 2017, he was awarded the Prix Meret Oppenheim by the Federal Office of Culture. In 2023, together with Karin Sander, he represented Switzerland with the exhibition *Neighbors* at the 18th Venice Architecture Biennale.

Image Credits

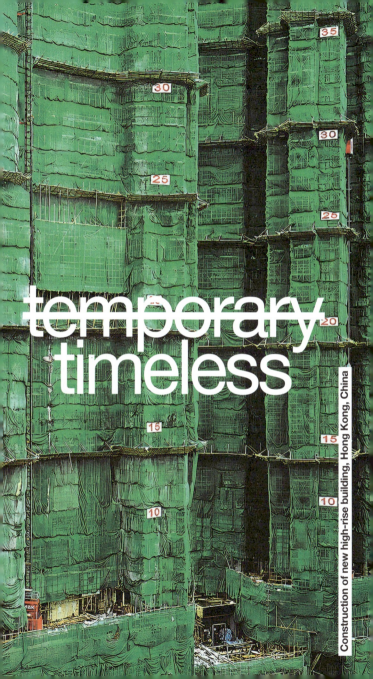

~~temporary~~
timeless

Construction of new high-rise building, Hong Kong, China

radical
without
manifesto

Reconstruction of Lenin's Mausoleum during winter, Moscow, Russia

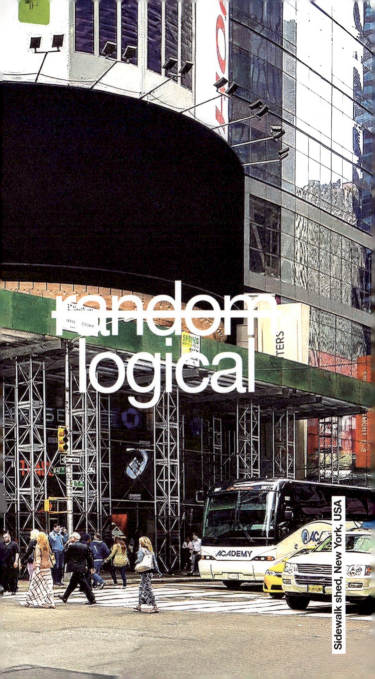

random
logical

Sidewalk shed, New York, USA

alien
natural

Agricultural net over vegetable fields, Haute-Savoie, France

scaleless
with
human
scale

Telescopic scaffolding posts for the construction of a new building, concrete floor slabs, Düsseldorf, Germany

excessive
urgent

Pontoons during the biggest religious festival in the world, Allahabad, India

primitive
futuristic

Bauprofile (outlines of a future building volume), Basel, Switzerland

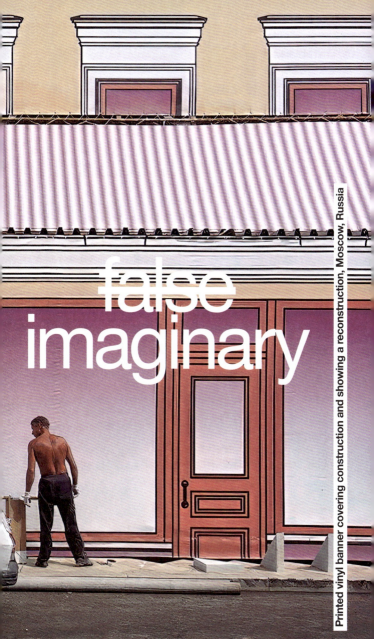

false

imaginary

Printed vinyl banner covering construction and showing a reconstruction, Moscow, Russia

Concept:
KOSMOS Architects:
Artem Kitaev
Leonid Slonimskiy

Copy editing:
Keonaona Peterson

Project management:
Baharak Tajbakhsh,
Sara Lusic-Alavanja,
Katharina Kulke

Production:
Amelie Solbrig

Layout coordination:
Irina Slonimskaya

Layout design
and typesetting:
Ksenia Dubrovskaya

Paper:
Agrippina Offset, 120 gsm

Printing:
Gutenberg Beuys
Feindruckerei GmbH

Image Editing:
prints professional

Library of Congress Control Number: 2024947791

Bibliographic information published by the German National Library
The German National Library lists this publication in the Deutsche
Nationalbibliografie; detailed bibliographic data are available on the
Internet at http://dnb.dnb.de.

ISBN 978-3-0356-2865-4
e-ISBN (PDF) 978-3-0356-2868-5

© 2025 Birkhäuser Verlag GmbH, Basel
Im Westfeld 8, 4055 Basel, Switzerland
Part of Walter de Gruyter GmbH, Berlin/Boston

9 8 7 6 5 4 3 2 1

MIX
Paper | Supporting
responsible forestry
FSC
www.fsc.org   FSC® C009051

www.birkhauser.com

Questions about General
Product Safety Regulation
productsafety@degruyterbrill.com